COOL TOOLS

by Lisa Trumbauer

STECK-VAUGHN
A Harcourt Company

www.steck-vaughn.com

wrench

Tools help you in many ways.

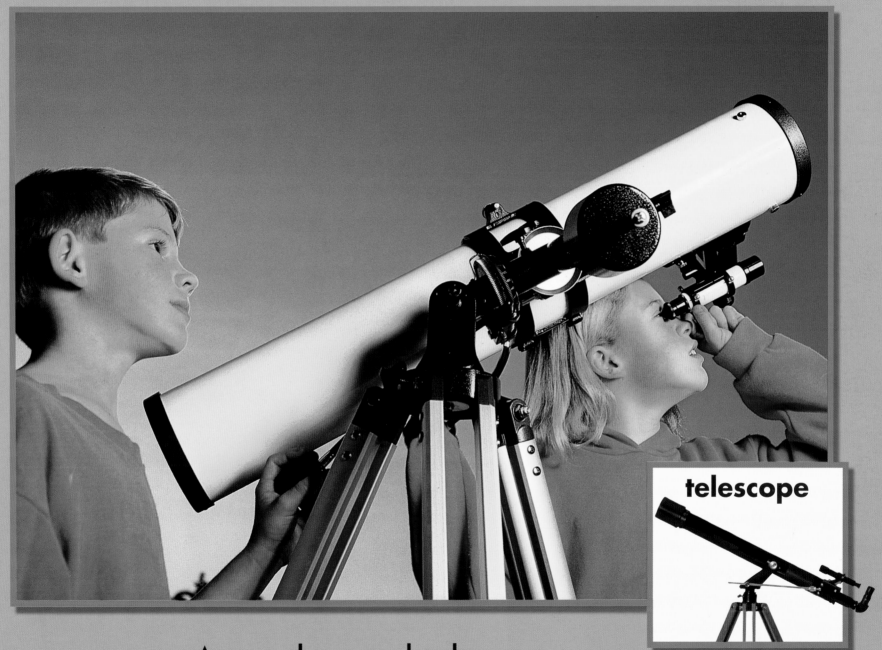

telescope

A tool can help you see.

stethoscope

A tool can help you hear.

computer

A tool can help you learn.

racing wheelchair

A tool can help you move.

watering can

A tool can help you work.

snorkel

A tool can help you breathe.